15 Baby Name Tips

Picking a name for your new baby boy or girl is one of the most important decisions you will have to face. Remember that the name is what identifies your baby for the rest of his or her life, so choose wisely!

1. The baby name should have a positive connotation for you.

The baby name should be pleasant and meaningful. A baby name has a strong first impression. Your baby's name reflects how you picture your baby as an adult. If you imagine that he may become an athletic person, you might select a name, which reflects physical strength and athleticism.

2. The baby first name's rhythm should match the last name.

As a tip, the number of syllables in the name should not match the number of syllables in the last name. Say the first, middle and last name several times to test the rhythm. Say the first name and last name together, too. Also, be conscious of what the first name and last name together say. If you have a common or easy to pronounce last name (i.e. Smith, Jones, Brown), you might find that an unusual or long first name can complement the last name nicely.

Or as one web visitor put it, a long or unusual first name "spices up" the whole name. Examples include Dakota Smith, Lucinda Brown and Sharona Flynn.

3. Check the pronunciation and spelling of the baby's name.

If you use an unusual pronunciation, your child will need to continually correct it. On the other hand, if the name is common, an unusual spelling will distinguish your child. Another factor is the ability to find personalized items. Unusual spellings will mean you have to special order or do without the personalized item.

4. The initials should not spell anything undesirable.

Check the first initial of the first and last name. Do they stand for anything? How about when you include all the middle name(s)?If the initials are not satisfactory, then the first and middle names can be switched. The child can still use the middle name on a day by day basis. For example, the name Paul Ivan Goldstein has the initials POG or Richard Alexander Thompson RAT.

5. Honor a family member.

Does your family have a tradition of picking names from the family tree? If this is important to you by all means stick with your family's tradition. Just remember, it is your decision so no one should have a final say on the name except you and your partner. Don't let family member by using their name as a middle name.

6. Combine names to create a new baby name.

You can choose two or more words to create a unique baby name. By separating each word into syllables and combining the syllables, you can create new baby names. You can even scramble a word to create a new baby name. For example, Sarita can come from combining the names Sam and Rita.

7. Be conscious of nicknames and variations.

Are you prepared to hear your child called by a nickname? Andrew will inevitably become "Andy" some of the time, even if you insist on the formal name. If you like the potential nicknames associated with the name you choose, well and good. But if you have strong feelings against them, think about choosing another name with nicknames you like better or consider names without commonly used nicknames such as "Eric" or "Mary".

8. Practice the baby's name and hear how it feels.

You will say this name thousands of times. You will say lovingly and in anger. You will whisper it when the child is asleep and yell it when dinner is ready.

9. Avoid letter redundancy between names.

Often, first last names with the same first letter do not sound well together. Also, if the last name ends with a vowel, the first name usually should not. The first name should not end with syllable that rhymes with the first syllable of the last name. For example, Angela Anna has quite a few letter A's.

10. Consider the baby name's meaning.

You may want to consider the importance of the baby name's. Even if this is not important to you. It may be important to your child.

11. Is an odd baby name a good thing?

Think twice before choosing an odd baby name. Research suggests kids with odd names are teased more by peers and are overall less socialized. But if your family is full of bravado and energy, odd baby names may be a great thing.

12. Baby names are cyclical.

Baby names which were once considered old fashioned will often come back into style. "Isaac" was a seldom used baby name for a long time, but has recently come back into fashion.

13. When to avoid celebrity baby names.

Some celebrities can become so much larger than life, their name becomes one you may not want to use for your baby names. We may never see many people naming their children Elvis or Cher.

14. Baby names using the mother's maiden name.

If retaining the mother's maiden name is important, and you do not like hyphenating last names, try using the maiden name as the first name or middle name. Many maiden names not be best suited for a first name, but will often make a great middle name.

15. When your baby is born.

There are so many things to consider! When your baby is born, you realize it's all a matter of feeling, not logic. And your feelings and your partner's matter more than any opinion offered by friends or family. Stick with the name you genuinely love. And look forward to welcoming your child, its proud bearer.

Meaning of the first letters

The letter A

A = 1. A is both the first letter of the alphabet and the first vowel. It represents the head.

Determination, enterprise, courage and strength of mind: you love adventures and experiments. You aim to fulfill your fantasies. In order to be more successful, rely more on friends and relatives.

A as the first vowel in a name means the person has a strong interest in life in general, and possesses an independent nature. When another A appears in the name is brings with it the quality of being level-headed and having the ability to think problems through. When three or more A's appear in the name, this can tip the scales toward selfishness.

The negative A can be a critical and skeptical individual, looking down upon the efforts of others from their lofty place of self-righteousness.

The letter B

B = 2. B is the second letter if the alphabet and represents the emotions. It is not a particularly strong letter in the physical plane, and can be influenced easily by others.

Super sensitive: you are shy, close and avoid noise parties. You have a good taste for luxury. You believe your partner is obliged to prove every day her/his feelings for you.

A love of domesticity, peace and quiet. A feminine B has a naturally motherly nature, while the male B has a love of nature and life in the country. They both feel a strong need for partnership, and have a strong dislike to being on their own. A negative B can be quite selfish, concerned with themselves and what they san get. They san also become greedy and possessive.

The letter C

C = 3 and is the third letter of the alphabet. It represents energy.

C is good-humored, extravagant and dexterous. The C is a natural talker, a born orator, with an intuitive and creative talent for eloquence. The C loves to be the organizer, and can be quite impulsive. You have infinite belief in your own abilities and you can cope with every challenge.

A negative C can be shameless, negligent, careless and unscrupulous.

The letter D

D = 4 and is the 4th letter of the alphabet. It represents balance and organization.

Sense of duty: in most cases, you are dependable, unless you are carried away by some stupid idea and decide to follow it blindly. You find it hard to express your feelings. You do not noisy meetings and have intensified sense of the true values in life.

The negative D can be stubborn, unyielding and uncompromising in its way of looking at situations. Push it far enough, and the negative D can easily be described as pig-headed.

The letter E

E = 5 and is both the fifth letter of the alphabet and the second vowel. It is a strong letter, representing communication.

Skilful, intellectual, imaginative and good-humored: everybody likes you for your sense or humor and optimism and admire you for taking such good care of your family.

E as the first vowel in a name points toward an interesting and event filled life. A person with 3 or more E's in their name can be nervous and temperamental, especially if E is the first vowel. A negative E can be irresponsible, unreliable and flirtatious.

The letter F

F = 6 and is the sixth letter of the alphabet. It is a letter representing love.

Domesticated and home-loving. F is friendly, a planner, comforting and loyal. It is very easy for the F to carry a strong sense of family responsibility. The family is the most important thing for her/him.

A negative F can easily spend a lot of their time being sad, depressed and anxious; feeling a vague sense of unease, even while sitting in the midst of plenty.

The letter G

G = 7 and is the seventh letter of the alphabet. G represents mysticism and religion.

Purposeful, orderly, inventive and instinctive. G can become quite involved with acting conventionally. Your exceptional business flair enables you to succeed in the business sphere and reach the top of the hierarchy.

The negative G loves to do things its own way. They heartily dislike advice. G can also be a doubter, and hard to convince of anything beyond its own, cherished opinions.

The letter H

H = 8 and is the eighth letter of the alphabet. It represents creativity and power.

H is, by nature, successful, self-contained, and a natural money maker. It has a strong connection with the earth, and is a lover of nature. Instead of troubling you, competition motivates you even more in order to achieve your goals. Your talent of predicting the events you from being surprised unpleasantly.

A negative H will be quite possessive, self-absorbed and greedy.

The letter I

I = 9 and is the ninth letter of the alphabet, as well as being the third vowel. It represents law.

I is genteel, impulsive, elegant and has warmth of heart. I is an inspirational letter.
Though you are kind, sensitive and friendly, with you is not always easy.

I as the first vowel in a name describes a person who is interested in the arts, science and drama. A negative I can be timid, nervous and quick to become angry, or fearful. When coming from the negative aspect of their nature, I's are easily offended.

The letter J

J = 10/1 and is the tenth letter of the alphabet.
J represents aspiration.

Cleaver, truthful, creative and helpful. J is
warm-hearted, well-meaning and reliable. You
find
it very hard to make your life choice.

A negative J can be lazy, listless, dull and
lethargic because they have no goal in life.

The letter K

K = 11/2, and as the eleventh letter of the
alphabet, K represents extremes. This is the
first of the Master Numbers.

K has a somewhat unyielding attitude to life
and other people. Yet it is sensitive, vigorous
and creative. K sees itself as an authority
figure. You are characterized with incredible
pragmatism and strong adaptability to
circumstances.

The letter L

L = 12/3 is the twelfth letter of the alphabet. L
represents action.

L is loyal, has a natural balance, and is a good
manager, along with having a kind disposition

and an intellectual mind. In love, you strive not to give yourself out without receiving anything in return.

A negative L can be accident-prone, being especially vulnerable to tripping and falling.

The letter M

M = 13/4 and is the thirteenth letter of the alphabet. M represents spirituality.

M has patience, is industrious, courageous and domesticated. The first letter of your name attracts happiness and activates your creative talent. You are capable of getting in contact with different people and make them like you.

The negative M is kind-of hasty, and behaves impatiently, or without thinking. They can also be bad tempered, and quick to anger.

The letter N

N = 14/5 and is the fourteenth letter of the alphabet. N represents imagination.

N is very certain of itself, as a writer and spokesman. N is imaginative and loves pleasure; especially when indulging the senses. Be careful with your excessive suspiciousness human nature. They can stop your from finding a soul-mate.

A negative N can be envious, covetous and jealous, with can cause divorce or separation (in both business and personal relationships), if it is taken to extremes.

The letter O

O = 15/6. It is both the fifteenth letter of the alphabet and the fourth vowel. O represents patience.

O brings, and carries, a sense of responsibility. It is knowledgeable and intellectual. And it can, under treating conditions, become moral to the point of being solemn. You can complicate your life and provoke people's disapproval by behaving in an eccentric and provoking way to them.

O as the first vowel in a name reveals a frank, methodical person who has respect for law and order in everything. A negative O should guard against jealousy and learn not to wear his or her heart on the sleeve.

The letter P

P = 16/7 and is the sixteenth letter of the alphabet. It represents power.

P is shrewd, thoughtful, talented, expressive and influential. Your sense of responsibility and discretion make you a prefect business partner.

A negative P is usually possessive, self-absorbed and with little time or sympathy for anyone else or their problems.

The letter Q

Q = 17/8. As the seventeenth letter of the alphabet, Q represents originality.

Q has a resolute energy, is enigmatic and difficult to analyze. Q has a determined personality, it is intense, and is a natural leader. Born adventurous, you are intuitive and too self-confident.

Negative Q's are rather boring people, especially when they talk too much. They are inclined to become extremely self-centered.

The letter R

R = 18/9 and is the eighteenth letter of the alphabet. R represents possibilities.

Enthusiastic, patient and even-tempered. R is stable, hard-working, warm hearted and compassionate.

A negative R is prone to mislaying or losing their possessions, and tends to be somewhat irritable, emotionally touchy and a bit of a miser. It is easy to aggravate a negative R, and to experience their rather short temper. Arrogance and pride can play trick on you and make you fail.

The letter S

S = 19/1 and is the nineteenth letter of the alphabet. It represents beginnings.

S in endowed with strong feelings, and is capable of lots of effort. Attractive, and with an easy magnetism for money and finances. S brings new beginnings. S is, by nature, successful, self-contained, and a natural money maker.

A negative S may experience many endeavors and failures during their life time. They are inclined to act impulsively and without reflecting on past experiences.

The letter T

T = 20/2 and is the twentieth letter of the alphabet. T represents growth.

T means action as well, emotion and restlessness. It is moral and religious; it has determination and is a builder. There is a natural authority to T, and it is creative. T is a very good-natured, clever and a true friend.

Negative T's are over-emotional, and easily influenced by the opinions of the opinions of others. They need to learn self-control in their thoughts, words deeds.

The letter U

U = 21/3. U is both the twenty-first letter of the alphabet and the fifth and last true vowel. It represents accumulation.

U is clever and shrewd, as well as being a collector and gatherer. A fascinating character, yet hard to know. U is lucky, and it never forgets an injury, or a good deed done. You are very sensitive and you easily get disappointed.

With U as the first vowel in a name, the person it represents is capable of understanding a great deal. It also gives the ability to formulate plans and carry them out. Negative U's can be selfish, indecisive and very acquisitive.

The letter V

V = 22/4 and is the twenty-second letter of the alphabet. It represents construction.

V is very honest and truthful, reliable and loyal. The V is gregarious, practical, industrious, sensitive and has very firm beliefs. He is also a very good friend.

A negative V can be very impractical and extremely unpredictable.

The letter W

W = 23/5 and it is the twenty-third letter of the alphabet. It represents self-expression.

W is persistent and full of purpose. It can be hard to know, and at the same time, is charming and sociable. W is naturally attractive, affable and with imagination. People admire you because you can control yourself in crisis and when you begin some work, you finish it good.

A negative W is way too fond of taking risks and cutting corners for his/her own good. This leads to many problems for themselves and others.

The letter X

X = 24/6. X is the twenty-fourth letter of the alphabet. It represents sexuality.

X is a born sensualist and, as such, is the natural seeker of pleasure. The X loves comfort, is easily led, and does not like to be tied down to commitment. X is an excellent money-maker and loves luxury.

A negative X can be a somewhat promiscuous person who is not only unfaithful in promises, but in their affections and commitments also.

The letter Y

Y = 25/7 and is the 25th letter of the alphabet. Y is one of the letters in the alphabet which, under certain conditions, is also used as a vowel. It represents freedom.

Y is very much the pioneer, and can't stand being held back. It is aesthetic, and enterprising. Y is also generous and compassionate.

Y is classed as a vowel when it takes on the sound of either an E or an I in a name. This depends on the pronunciation, and it is given the value of the sound it emulates. For example, E as in the name Yvonne or I in the name Lynda.

A negative Y is indecisive when faced with choice. This causes them to miss much of the happiness in life.

The letter Z

Z = 26/8 and, as the last letter in the alphabet, Z represents hope.

Z is trusting, compassionate, with a sense of consideration for other people. It is practical and down-to-earth, combined with common-sense and diplomacy. Z is very responsible person and good-hearted person.

A negative Z can be a very impatient, head-strong individual who needs to learn to think before acting or speaking.

Top 20 sexy boy names with analysis

1. Michael – Your name of Michael has given you very practical hard-working, systematic nature. You have a clever mind, a sense of responsibility, good business judgment, and an appreciation of the finer things of life. You are serious minded and in your younger years you have more mature interest than other your age.

2. William – The name of William gives you very individual, reserved, serious nature. You prefer to be alone with your own thoughts, rather than in the company of others. Home and family mean a great deal to you and it is natural that you should desire the security of a peaceful, settled home environment.

3. Christopher – The name of Christopher incorporates a potential aptitude for concentration and patient, logical thought along mechanical or scientific lines. You gravitate to situations where you have stability and the opportunity to make slow step progress. This name creates a deliberate and methodical way of thinking and speaking; it takes you time to learn

but, once you have mastered a subject, you do not forget it.

4. Matthew – The name of Matthew gives you a generous quality to your nature. This name causes you to be somewhat too concerned with the personalities, problems, and other people, but you must guard carefully against giving more than you receive or you will find yourself doing without because you have helped someone else.

5. Kyle – The name of Kyle creates a very aggressive and independent nature, one with big ambitions, giving you original, progressive, large-scale ideas, salesmanship and promotional ability as well as the excellent business judgment, which enables you to gain the financial accumulation to which you feel entitled.

6. Jason – The name of Jason has given you the desire to meet and mix socially and to create congenial circumstances for everyone. You are good at sales work and you could do well because of your friendly personality, interest in people, and desire to please. Your ideas can be very original and inventive.

7. Brad – The name of Brad has made you serious-minded, responsible, and stable. You love the security of a home and family, you are fond of children, and, as a parent you would be fair and understanding. You have a diplomatic and tactful manner and possess a charming, easy-going nature which puts

people at ease. People are drawn to you because they feel that you are patient, kind, understanding, and responsive.

8. Daniel –As Daniel you have a great love of nature and the out-of-doors, and could have a desire to be in an occupation, which takes you outdoors and involves you with the earth. You are not overly ambitions, preferring instead to seek stable, settled conditions which are adequate to meet your responsibilities. You like to be your own boss and you are capable of handling responsibilities for others.

9. Joey – The name of Joey has given you a very imaginative, creative mind. You always have new ideas, but too often, they are for an easy way out of a difficulty, or an easy way of making money. You seek chance in order to have the opportunity for travel, new experience, and new friends and associates. You desire independence and freedom from the authority and interference of others.

10.   Joshua – Your name of Joshua gives you the ability to be creative along practical lines and endeavor. Your personal appearance is important to you, for you desire to make a good impression on others. Your pleasant manner attracts people to you with there are capable of offering practical advice, thought you would probably not follow such advice yourself.

11.   David – Your first name of David has given you a very systematic nature. In reaching your goals, you are very independent and resourceful, patient and determined. You can be very positive and definite in your own ideas and opinions. Also, this name does not incorporate qualities that enable you to be diplomatic and to compromise.

12.   Dylan – The name of Dylan creates a very passive, easy-going, friendly nature. You love people and desire to get along with everyone you meet. Your creative nature and ambitions drive you to pursuer success to the extent that you jeopardize your personal well-being. People are drawn to you because they feel that you are patient, kind, understanding, and responsive.

13.   Ryan – The name of Ryan has created a most expressive nature, idealistic and inspirational, driven a strong inner urge to be of service in some way that would up lift humanity. You would be successful in any position dealing with the public as you have a diplomatic and tactful manner and possess a charming, easygoing nature which puts people at ease. You love the security of a home and family.

14.   Nick – Your first name of Nick makes you extremely generous. You have a bubbling, spontaneous nature and a happy-go-lucky outlook which helps smooth the pathway of life. Also you are

sympathetic to the needs of others. Your spontaneous expression stands you in good stead during arguments or debates. You are fun and party loving person.

15.   Paul – Your name of Paul gives you self-assurance, independence, and confidence. You have depth of mind and the ability to concentrate and to follow a line of thought to a logical conclusion. Your love of challenging the concepts of others invariably leads you to create your own ideas and to pioneer new of thought. Your strong characteristic of individuality qualifies you as a leader.

16.   Justin – Your name of Leo makes you quick-minded, versatile, and very expressive. You have the ability to create a favorable first impression, and so you could do well in the field of sales promotion or entertainment. You are adaptable and creative in responding to new situation. You like to finish what you start without interuptions, and also to have everything in its place and properly organized.

17.   Jacob – The name of Jacob creates a quiet, systematic, and technical nature and a clever, inventive mind, attentive to detail. You are attracted to working outdoors in nature, where you would experience the peace and serenity you so much desire. You are inclined to be quiet, reserved, patient, and conservative, preferring to test and prove everything to your own satisfaction before committing.

18.	Anthony – Your first name of Anthony has given you an expressive, diplomatic, and gracious nature. You have a good appreciation of material values, business ability, and skill in organizing and managing others. You have very expensive tastes, and your desires could well exceed your initiative in providing for them thought your own efforts. Personal appearance is important to you. You are always well-groomed yourself

19.	James – While your name of James gives you an intense desire to be of service to others, it brings out a practical, technical nature, and you become involved in fussy little details that detract from the fulfilment of your greater ideals. You are a very patient person and will work hard one step at a time to accomplish your goals. Not interested in large undertakings, you are content to live from day to day to save for your future. Always budgeting carefully, you do not believe in frivolous spending.

20.	Max – The name of Max crates a very aggressive and independent nature, one with big ambitions, giving you original, progressive, large-scale ideas, salesmanship ability as well as the excellent business judgment, which enable you to gain the financial accumulation to which you feel entitled. You are seldom satisfied and are always seeking something new. You like to be your own boss and you are capable of handing responsibilities for others.

Top 20 sexy girl names with analysis

1. Emma – The name of Emma creates a restless, creative nature that takes you into many ventures. Yours is a versatile, musical, artistic, but independent nature and you must have the freedom to express your creative ideas and abilities to be happy. This name also gives you a love of name and family, and as a parent, you would likely be fair and understanding.
2. Jessica – Your name of Jessica has given you a responsible, expressive, inspirational and friendly personality. Self-confidence has made it easy for you to meet people and you are well-like for yours spontaneous, happy ways. You sincerely like people and do often experience loneliness.
3. Christine – As Christine you seek change, travel new opportunities, and new challenges. Your active, restless nature demands action and dislike system and monotony. As you are versatile and

capable, you could do any job well, although you would not like to do menial tasks. You are not afraid to risk a gamble as the name gives you much self-confidence.

4. Michelle – Your name of Michelle has made you a hard worker with a meticulous sense of detail. You have a great deal of patience and independence, and you can be relied upon to complete your undertakings. You are stable, trustworthy and home loving. You resist change.

5. Ashley – Your name of Ashley has given you a rather quiet, reserved, serious nature. You have sensitivity and appreciation for the finer and deeper things of life, the beauties of nature, music, art and literature. The people who mean the most to you are those who can offer you intellectual companionship.

6. Nicole – The name of Nicole has created a congenial nature with the desire to associate in friendship and understanding both socially and in the business world. You have a clever, quick mind, with the ability to accomplish a great deal in a short period of time, although it is not easy for you to systematize your efforts.

7. Jennifer – The name of Jennifer leads you to assume considerable responsibility and to prefer to work independently, without direction or interference from other because you have very definite ideas of

your own. This name does make you quite direct and straight – to-the-point.

8. Victoria – The name of Victoria has given you a quick-minded, sensitive nature. It gives you a clever, creative ability in art, music, singing or drama and an appreciation for refined surrounding. As you respond to love and encouragement from others, your romantic and dreamy nature can lead you into love affairs.

9. Angelina – Your name of Angelina has made you versatile and creative. There is hardly anything you cannot do if put your mind to it but a driving urge leads you to one experience after another, seldom finishing what you start. As soon as a challenger is met, boredom sets in, and you yearn for another experience.

10. Carmen – Your mane of Carmen makes you very idealistic and generous. You want to assume responsibilities and to look after people, however, you can become too involved in other people's problems and tend to worry. You desire a settled home and family life, and are expressive and attentive to your loved ones.

11. Samantha – Your name of Samantha has given you the desire for the best that money can buy: good clothes, and refined surroundings, all the finer things of life, although you might be inclined to get things though the influence of others rather than though

hard work. You always strive to create a good impression.

12. Natalie – Your name of Natalie has given you a desire for self-expression and for positions that allow contact with people, free from the restrictions and monotony into which you are often drawn. You strive to different and have the self-confidence to implement your ideas because have the perseverance necessary to see something though, despite obstacles. Although you meet new people easily, it is not easy to you to maintain a relaxed, harmonious relationship.

13. Stephanie – Your name of Stephanie contributes sensitive, creative and idealistic qualities to your nature that could be expressed in a variety of literary or artistic fields. Although mentally quick and intuitive, you experience a lack of fluency in verbal expression in responding. Your emotional feeling are easily affected and you will be always involved in other people's problems as a result of your overly sympathetic nature.

14. Sydney – The name of Sydney creates a very versatile and creative nature. You are quick-minded and have the freedom of expression to mix easily with people. You seek change in order to have the opportunity for travel, new friends and associates. As you are naturally talkative, you find it easy to

meet and make friends with many people. This name inclines you to be sympathetic and generous to those in difficult and unfortunate circumstances.

15.   Naomi – As Naomi you have a great love of nature and the out-of-doors. All the finer things of life and beauties of nature are an inspiration to you and you are attracted to the mysteries of nature. The average person would never realize the true depth of your nature.

16.   Kimberly – The name Kimberly gives you a strongly independent and highly creative nature, with drive and ambition to have experiences and accomplish things out of the ordinary. You are friendly, sociable and charming person. While you find it easy to meet and mix, and can appear agreeable and compromising in conversation, you can become unbending and forceful if pressed too far.

17.   Vanessa – Your first name of Vanessa has created a deep, sensitive, refined nature with an intelligent mind. You can be lifted by beauty in all forms and are at the most creative when inspired. Your expressive, affectionate nature responds quickly though your feelings, but you must guard against being possessive and jealous.

18.   Lindsay – Your name of Lindsay creates a desire for association with people and new experience. This name has given you a gregarious personality

and a quick-thinking, creative, and versatile nature, but one that is very emotional. You like to make your own decision and to be the master of your domain. You feel a limitation in your own expression when it is necessary to reach another through tact and understanding.

19.　　Chantel – Your name of Chantel makes you very idealistic and generous, with the strong desire to uplift humanity leading you into situations where you can express your desire to serve others. You have a serious desire to understand the heart and mind of everyone, and could be very effective in a career or in volunteer work where you are handing people and serving in a humanitarian way.

20.　　Elizabeth – The name of Elizabeth gives you leadership qualities and you are seldom happy in positions where you must direction from others. Material and financial success are the focus of your interest. You have a very independent, practical, analytical nature with skillful business abilities. Whatever you undertake, you have the patience and determination to do well. Difficulty in accepting advice or admitting that you may have a mistake causes you to appear to be stubborn and set in your ways.

Name teams

Names with "Strong" meanings

Abd – Al – Aziz Atabic (m)	Servant of the powerful
Abdul Arabic (m)	Servant
Alcippe Latin (f)	Mighty Mare
Aziz Arabic (m)	Powerful, Great
Berk Turkish (m)	Film, Steadfast
Carlisle Old English (m)	Strong as the Shining One
Gabriel Hebrew (m)	Strength of God
Ikaika Hawaiian (m)	Strong
Iphigenia Greek (f)	Mythical Creature
Jelani African (m)	Powerful Might
Jirair Armenian (m)	Strong, Hardworking
Ken Gaelic (m)	Helmeted chief
Kenji Japanese (m)	Strong, Healthy Second Son
Magnhild Norwegian (f)	Powerful Battle

Metin	Strong
Turkish (m)	
Valentine	Good health
Latin (m)	
Valerius	Strength, Valor
Ancient Roman (m)	
Waltraud	Rule strength
Teutonic (f)	

Name with " Brave " Meanings

Archibald	Bold Prince	Anglo
– Saxon (m)		
Baldric	Bold, Powerful,Brave	
Old English (m)		
	Ruler	
Baldwin	Brave Friend	
German (m)		
Bernard	Bold as a Bear	
German (m)		
Burkhard	Brave Protector	
German (m)		
Eckhard	Brave Swordsman	
German (m)		
Everard	Brave Boar	
Old English (m)		
Gebhard	Brave Gift	
German (m)		
Gerard	Spear, Brave	
Old German (m)		
Giffard	Brave Gift	
Old English (m)		

Hartmann   Brave Man
     German (m)
Hartmut   Brave Mind
     German (m)
Howard   Guardian of the
     English (m)
                  home, watchman
Kenelm   Brave Helmet   Old
English (m)
Leonard   Lion – hearted   Old
German (m)
Nanna   Graceful one
        Hebrew (f)
Wyatt   Little warrior, water
     Old English (m)

Names with " Intelligent " Meanings

Albert   Noble, Bright
     German (m)
Bert   Fortress
     Old English (m)
Bertram   Bright
     German (m)
Berthold   Glorious ruler
     Teutonic (m)
Bertha   Brilliant, Illuminated
     German (f)
                        Fame
Bilge   Wise
     Turkish (f)
Clara   Clear, Illuminated
     Latin (f)

Clarice	Clear, Illuminated	
French (f)		
Colbert	Cool, Bright	
Old English (m)		
Cuthbert	Bright Fame	
Old English (m)		
Delbert	Bright Valley	Old
English (m)		
Eirian	Illuminating Beauty	
Welsh (f)		
Engelbert	Bright as an Angel	
German (m)		
Frode	Wisdom	
Danish (m)		
Gilbert	Bright Pledge	
Dutch (m)		
Gladwyn	Bright Friend	Old
English (m)		
Herbert	Bright Army Ruler	
French (m)		
Hubert	Brilliant Heart and	
Mind Dutch (m)		
Kalea	Bright, Clear	
Hawaiian (f)		
Kunibert	Brave, Bright	
German (m)		
Lambert	Wealthy in land	Latin
(m)		
Leocadia	Clear, Shining	
Spanish (f)		
Noga	Bright	
Hebrew (f)		
Norbert	Blonde hero	
German (m)		

Robert   Bright, famous
      Old English (m)
Savio   Intelligent
      Italian (m)
Shannon   Wise, River
      Irish (f)
Shirley   Bright Meadow
      Old English (f&m)
Sumati   Wisdom
      Hindu (f&m)
Ziv   Very bright
      Hebrew (f&m)

Names with " Happy " Meanings

Abigel   God is Joy
        Modern English (f)
Aasher   Blessed, Happy
      Modern English (f)
Aliza   Joyful
      Hebrew (f)
Fortunato   Fortunate
      Italian (m)
Freyde   Joy
      Yiddish (f)
Gay   Happy   Old
English (f)
Gilah   Joyful
      Hebrew (f)
Gioconda   Joyful
      Italian (f)
Happy   Joyful
      English (f&m)

Joy	Joy	Old English
Letitia	Joy, Gladness	Latin (f)
Liron	Joyful Song	Hebrew (m&f)
Meriwether	Merry Weather	Middle English (m&f)
Rada	Joyful	Czechoslovakian (f)
Radomil	Joyful, Favored	Bulgarian (m)
Simcha	Joyful	Hebrew (f&m)
Winston	Joy Stone	Old English (m)

Names with " Beautiful " Meanings

Alana	Attractive
Gaelic (f)	
Anwen	Stunningly Beautiful
Welsh (f)	
Aoibheann	Beautiful Patina
Gaelic (f)	
Beau	Beautiful, Handsome
French (m)	
Beaumont	Beautiful Mountain
French (m)	
Beauregard	Beautiful, Handsome View
French (m)	

Bellanita	Gracious Beauty	
French (f)		
Belle	Beautiful	
French (f)		
Branwen	White, Fair, Blessed Hill	
Welsh (f)		
Calanthe	Beautiful Flower	
Old English (f)		
Calogero	Elderly Beauty	
Italian (m)		
Caoimhe	Beautiful	Celtic
(f)		
Coinneach	Handsome	
Gaelic (f)		
Erianthe	Sweet as Many Flowers	
Greek (f)		
Grazyna	Beautiful	
Lithuanian (f)		
Graziella	Graceful Beauty	
Italian (f)		
Isolde	Beautifuk	Celtic
(f)		
Jaffe	Beauty	
Hebrew (f)		
Jamil	Attractive	
Arabic (m)		
Keefe	Handsome, Beloved	
Gaelic (m)		
	Handsome, Gentle	
Kevin	Beloved	
Gaelic (f)		
Linda	Beautiful	
Spanish (f)		
Mabelle	Lovable, Beautiful	
Old English (f)		

MacKenzie	Son of wise leader	
Gaelic (m&f)		
Nava	Beauty	
Hebrew (f)		
Rosabella	Beautiful Rose	
Italian (f)		
Sigrid	Winning adviser	Old
Norse (f)		
Zuri	Attractive	
African (f)		

Name with " Lucky " Meanings

Felix	Happy	Latin
(m)		
Fortunato	Fortunate	
Italian (m)		
Fortune	Fortunate	Old
English (f)		
Madoc	Blessed	
Welsh (m)		
Prosper	Prosperous, Successful	
French (m)		
Shreya	Auspicious	
Hindu (f)		
Xiang	Fragrant Flight	
Chinese 9 (m&f)		

Name with " Generous " Meanings

Aimo   Generous
        Finnish (m)
Charity   Charity, Kind   Latin
(f)
Ithel   Generous Prince
        Welsh (m)
Karim   Giving, Noble
        Arabic (m)
Theodosius   Gift of God
        Greek (m)

Name with " Royal " Meanings

Abd – Al – Malik   Servant of the King
        Arabic (m)
Almira   Princess
        Old English (f)
Armel   Prince
        French (m)
Basil   Royal, Brave   Greek
(m)
Donald   World Leader
        Old English (m)
Edric   Blessed, Pwerful Ruler
        Old English (m)
Elric   Elf Ruler   Old
English (m)
Emyr   King
        Welsh (m)

Eric	Ever Powerful Ruler
Scandinavian (m)	
Fitzroy	Son of the King
Old English (m)	
Frederick	Peaceful, Powerful Ruler
Old English (m)	
Friedhold	Peacedul Ruler
German 9 (m)	
Gruffydd	Prince
Welsh (m)	
Harold	Army Ruler
Old English (m)	
Henry	Ruler of the Home
Old English (m)	
Idris	Enthusiastic Prince
Welsh (m)	
Ithel	Generous Prince
Welsh (m)	
Lareyna	Queen
Spanish (f)	
Leroy	King
Old French (m)	
Reagan	Little King
Gaelic (m&f)	
Regina	Queen
Latin (f)	
Reine	Queen Latin
(f)	
Rex	King
Latin (m)	
Rhiannon	A mythological nymph
Welsh (f)	
Rhodri	King Wheel
Welsh (m)	

Roald   Fame power
      Teutonic (m)
Ryan   Little King
      Gaelic (m&f)
Sarah   Princess
      Hebrew (f)
Torvald   Thor's Ruler
      Scandinavian (m)
Walter   Army Ruler
        Old German (m)
Xerxes   Prince
      Persian (m)
Zoltan   Life, Sultan
        Hungarian (m)

Name with " Religious " Meanings

Abd – Allah   Servant of God
      Arabic (m)
Abiel   God is My Father
      Hebrew (m)
Abijah   Yahweh is My God
      Hebrew (m)
Abimael   God is My Father
      Hebrew (m)
Adalia   Yahweh is Just
      Hebrew (m)
Adonai   My Lord
      Hebrew (m)
Adonijah   Lord is Yahweh
      Herbrew (m)
Amariah   Yahweh Has Spoken
      Hebrew (m)

Ammiel My Kinsman is God
      Herbrew (m)
Anselm Divine Protection
      Old English (m)
Ansgar Spear god
      German (m)
Ariel Lion of God
      Herbrew (m&f)
Asbjorn Bear god
      Norwegian (m)
Azarel Helped by God
      Hebrew (m)
Beelzebub Fly Lord
      Hebrew (m)
Benaiah Yahweh has Created
      Hebrew (m)
Bethel House of God
      Hebrew (f)
Bethuel Man of God
      Hebrew (m)
Bithiah Yahweh's Daughter
            Hebrew (f)
Bogumil God's Favor
Polish (m)
Boguslaw Glory of God
      Polish (m)
Bohumir God is Peaceful
      Czechoslovakian (m)
Cedric Lord of Wars
      Old English (m)
Chibuzo God Leads
      African (m&f)
Cyriacus Of the Lord
      Ancient Roman (m)

Cyril   Lord
      Old English (m)
Daniel   God is My Judge
        Old English (m)
Delaiah   Drawn by Yahweh
     Hebrew (m)
Devdan   Gift of God
      Hindu (m)
Dominic   Belonging of God
    Old English (m)
Dorothea   Gift of God
     Dutch (f)
Eliezer   God is My Helper
       Hebrew (m)
Elihu   Yahweh is God
Hebrew (m)
Elijah   The Lord is My God   Old
English (m)
Elizabeth   Consecrated to God
    Old English (f)
Elkanah   Created by God
Hebrew (m)
Emmanuel   God is whit Us
Hebrew (m)
Gabriel   Strength of God
French (m)
Geoffrey   Peace of God   Old
English (m)
Goddard   Brave god   Old
Engilsh (m)
Godelieve   God's Love
     Dutch (m)
Godfrey   Peace of God   Old
English (m)

Godiva	Gift of God	
	Old English (f)	
Godwin	Friend of God	Old
English (m)		
Gotthold	God's Love	
German (m)		
Hananiah	Yahweh is Gracious	
Hebrew (m)		
Hazael	Sees God	
Hebrew (m)		
Ishmael	God Will Hear	Old
English (m)		
Israel	Wrestles With God	
Hebrew (m)		
Jessica	God Watches	
Old English (f)		
Jonathan	God Has Given	Old
English (m)		
Joshua	God Saves	
Old English (m)		
Mathew	Gift of God	
Old English (m)		
Osborn	Divine, Bear	
Old English (m)		
Raphael	God of God	
French (m)		
Theodore	Gift of God	
French (m)		
Timothy	To Honor God	Old
English (m)		
Zechariah	Remembered by God	Old
English (m)		

Name with " Flowery " Meanings

Anthony	Flower	Old
English (m)		
Blodeuyn	Blossom	
Welsh (f)		
Blossom	Flower bug	Old
English (f)		
Bluma	Flower	
Hebrew (f)		
Calanthe	Beautiful Flower	Old
English (f)		
Fioralba	Flower at Dawn	
Italian (f)		
Fiorella	Flower	
Italian (f)		
	Flourishing, Blooming	
Fiorenza	Prosperous	
Italian (f)		
Floriana	Gracious Flower	
Italian (f)		
Flower	Flower	
Old English (f)		
Iolanthe	Violet Flower	
Old English (f)		
Ornella	Blooming Ash Tree	
Italian (f)		
Rhosyn	Rose	
Welsh (f)		
Rosa	Rose	Latin
(f)		
Rosabella	Beautiful Rose	
Italian (f)		

Rosalia Italian (f)	Rose	
Rosalinda English (f)	Beautiful Rose	
Rosalyn English (f)	Beautiful Rose	Old
Rosamunda (f)	Pure Rose	Latin
Susanna English (f)	Lily	Old
Zahrah Atabic (f)	Blooming Flower	

Name with " Elfin " Meanings

Alfhild Norwegian (f)	Elf Battle	
Alfredia Modern English (f)	Elf Counselor	
Alfihar German (m)	Elf Army	
Alger German (m)	Elf Spear	Old
Alvin English (m)	Elf Friend	Old
Auberon English (m)	Noble, Elf Bear	Old
Aubrey English (m&f)	Elf Power	Old
Elric English (m)	Elf Wood	Old
Siofra (f)	Elf	Irish

Female names associated with " Flowers"

	Fresh and Sparking	
Amaryllis	Flower	
Old English		
Anemone	Wind Flower	
Greek		
April	4h Month, Blossoming	Latin
Camellia	Flowering Shrub	Old
English		
Celandine	Celandine Flower	Old
English		
Chrysanta	Chrysanthemum	Old
English		
Clover	Clover Flower	
Old English		
Daffodil	Daffodil Flower	Old
English		
	Flower Named for	
Dahlia	Botanist A. Dahl	
Hebrew		
Daisy	Daisy Flower	
Old English		
Eglantine	Sweetbrier	Old
English		
Flora	Flower	
Latin		
Gardenia	Tropical Flower	Old
English		

Heather	Flowering Shrub	Old English
Iris	Iris Flower	Greek
Ivy	Vine	Greek
Jasmine	Jasmine, Fragrant Flower	Persian
Lavender	Flower, Light Purple Color	Old English
Lily	Lily Flower	Latin
Linnea	Lime tree, national flower of Sweden	Norwegian
Lotus	Lotus Flower	Greek
Magnolia	Flower	French
Marigold	Golden Flower	Greek
Narcissa	Narcissus	Greek
Pansy	Pansy Flower	Old Englsih
Petunia	Petunia Flower	Latin
Primrose	Primrose Flower, meaning First Rose	Old English
Rose	Rose	French
Violet	Violet Flower	Latin
Zinnia	Zinnia Flower	Old English

Numerology and the Destiny Baby Number

It is time to reveal the secrets of your baby name using numerology! Probably, you have already chosen some baby names. Select one baby name and write it down. Now assign numbers to each letter using the chart below. The chart is read downwards so that 1 is A, J, S;
2 is B, K, T; etc.

1	2	3	4	5	6	7	8	9
A	B	C	D	E	F	G	H	I
J	K	L	M	N	O	P	Q	R
S	T	U	V	W	X	Y	Z	_

For example, I will use Amanda as a baby name. Now I assign numerical values to Amanda's full name using the chart.

AMANDA – 1 + 4 + 1 + 5 + 4 + 1

Now add all numbers together:

AMANDA = 16 or (7)

In numerology, 16 become 7 (1 + 6) . Most two – digit numbers get " broken down " in the same way. The only exceptions are the " master numbers " (11, 22) . When a master number appears in the final total, it can be read two ways (11, 22) .

As you can see from the above calculations, Amanda's name reduces to a 7 . In numerology, this particular combination provides the " Destiny Number " .

Let's check what Amanda's destiny number is! After that, choose a baby name and find irs secrets!

On the chart below is a quick interpretation of the numbers 1 through 9 and the two master numbers 11 and 22 . Enjoy!

Numbers Revealed!

1 – is ambitious, independent, self-confident, money-oriented, decisive, and stern.

2 – is supportive, diplomatic, analytical, responsible, careful, and domestic.

3 – is enthusiastic, optimistic, fun-loving, friendly, vigorous and holiday-maker.

4 – is practical, traditional, serious, spiritual, eccentric, and a bit of a loner.

5 – is adventurous, mercurial, sensual, good-hearted, powerful and fashionable.

6 – is kind-hearted, industrious, creative, well-bred, tenacious and sensitive.

7 – is clever, quick-minded, creative, curious, jealous and mysterious.

8 – is expressive, generous, artsy-craftsy, tactful, conversable and self-opinionated.

9 – is multi-talented, compassionate, global, athletic, stubborn and selfish.

11 – is enlightened, intense, high-strung, intuitive, smart and vindictive.
    (Also read the " lower " vibration of 2 above.)

22 – is goal-oriented, a global planner, inspired, good humored, and sociable.
    (Also read the " lower " vibration of 4 above.)

Numerology and Lucky Rich Baby Names

This time, numerology implies wealthy and not wealthy numbers. If the numbers in the following chart are with " $ " , they are the lucky rich numbers. This means, that if your baby name has " $ " numbers, she or he will be fortunate and well-to-do in life!

1$	2	3$	4	5$	6$	7$	8$
	9	10					
11$	12	13$	14	15$	16$	17$	18$
	19	20					
21$	22	23$	24$	25$	26	27	28
	29$	30					
31$	32$	33$	34	35$	36	37$	38*
	39$	40					
41$	42	43	44	45$	46	47$	48$
	49	50					
51	52$	53	54	55*	56	57$	58*
	59	60					
61*	62	63$	64	65$	66	67$	68$
	69	70					
71*	72*	73$	74	75*	76	77*	78*
	79	80					
81$							

Note! The numbers with "*" are extremely clever numbers. This means, that if your baby name has "*" , the baby will be genius! All the other numbers are good-natured numbers, which means that your baby will be good-hearted and sensitive!

To apply on baby name, I count how many letters in the name to determine if the name is lucky rich name or not. For example, I choose the name David Franklin Peterson.

FULL NAME	DAVID	FRANKLIN	PETERSON
LETTER COUNT	5	8	8

You can see that 5, 8 and 8 are Lucky Rich Numbers!

Now choose a baby name and check if it is Lucky Rich Name!

Five Fun Facts about Names

1. Every child has an official right to have a name. Article 24-3 of the U. N. International Covenant on Civil and Political Rights says so. Why was this declaration necessary? The U. N. recognized that children born into war zones, extreme poverty, and refugee camps may not have their births registered, making them especially vulnerable to all kinds of abuse.

2. The U. S. Census Bureau estimates that 88 000 different last names account for more than 90 percent of the 280 million people in the U. S. By contrast, China-with its population of more than 1 billion-has only 150 to 400 basic surnames. Clear proof of the diversity of America's melting-pot society.

3. When it comes to variety in names, girls rule. Again, according to the Census Bureau, approximately 90 percent of the U. S. population is covered by 4 275 different girls' names,
names, but only 1 219 different boys' names. Why so many fewer names for boys than for girls? It may be that boys' names are more tradition-bound, because boys are more likely to be named after a relative. Another possibility: Although this is changing, our society still

clings to the assumption that boys will eventually have to get " serious " jobs (and so need serious-sounding names), while girls won't, leaving more leeway for creativity, if not frivolity.

4. Anemonyms (a truly lovely word) are the names of winds and storms. Once a name has been associated with a violent hurricane, that name is retired. There will never be another Hurricane Hugo, for instance. The Weather Service also tries to pick names that ate easy to pronounce and culturally sensitive.

5. Toponyms are place names. Early U. S. names mirrored places in the old country (New England, for example), honored English royalty (Virginia, after Queen Elizabeth, known as the Virgin Queen), or celebrated the Pilgrims' survival (Providence). America itself, however, was named after Italian navigator and explorer Amerigo Vespucci in the early 16th century.

Asrology
Names for Every Month

January

January people are patient and reserved. They endure all the troubles with stoicism, and they share their inmost with difficulty even with those who are closest to them. January women are with a firm, man's character, secretive and independent. They are proud and highly appreciate
their independence. Family life with them is not easy because of their permanent aspiration after leadership, but they are devoted wives and are always ready to support their husbands. At that, women are expert cooks, but they don't like cleaning and do it perforce. January men are courageous and just people, they can be relied on in a difficult moment. They are decisive in their deeds, they often behave without considering those around them and they are inclined to unjustified risk. They are patronizing to people weaker than they are, they treat women with respect and they are capable of forgiving everything. They are proud and possess strong will. They are wonderful husbands. January children should have names with soft sounding aimed at neutralizing the excessive hardness of their nature and softening their pride. Appropriate names are:

Ashley, Melanie, Holly, Wendy, Selena,
Matthew, Anthony, Kyle, Samuel, Lucas.

February

February people are persistent, persevering and
too unbalanced, though unlike December ones
they are capable of exercising control over
themselves. Their nature is complicated,
unpredictable, they are subjected to nervous
collapses. They are very courageous and are not
afraid of difficulties. They make decisions fast,
indeed, they are sometimes incorrect. Unlike
January people they forgive insults with
difficulty, some of them are rancorous and
revengeful. They are not inclined to play noble
and magnanimous, they despise the weak.
They are too straightforward and egoistical. By
nature they are careerists, they are capable of
not particularly plausible deeds aimed at
attaining their objectives, they know to
manipulate people. It is inherent for them that
they go from one extreme to the other. They like
children and there are often more children in
their families. Appropriate names are:
Sebastian, Oliver, Robert, Edward, James,
Rebecca, Astrid, Deborah, Courtney, Sandra.

March

March people are very sensitive and
susceptible. They endure failure with difficulty
and this is why they slowly climb up the official
ladder. Although they show obstinacy and

persistence, this is often to their detriment. They are cowardly, indecisive, easily vulnerable. They consider that they do not go well on in life. It is not in vain that there are many ill-fared and envious amongst. March people. They strive after success all their lives but they remain unrecognized. If they manage to climb to the top of the glory in spite of that, this is usually not for long and falling down from there means collapse of all their hopes for them. Such allegedly spring people are self-centered and ambitious. They are irritable, waspish, and accept other people's successes as their own defeat. They are phlegmatic and heap up the people close to them with their endless complaints from fate. They are mistrustful, they believe in prejudice and they often turn to fortune-tellers. Men are grumbles, they are difficult to please and excessively squeamish. Women waste a lot of time for their dressing, they pay great attention to their appearance, they in front of the mirror for hours on end before leaving home. Such children had better be given names with hard sounding to add more decisiveness, tenacity to their nature so that the child could feel more confident in him or herself. Appropriate names are: Hillary, Virginia, Monica, Marta, Veronica, Aron, Scott, George, Trevor, Roland.

April

April people possess a firmer nature than March ones. They persistently pursue their goals, they are brave and decisive, regardless of the fact that do not always succeed themselves adequately. They are practical and sober-minded. They are excited in the material side of life. They are easily promoted in their jobs and they know what they want. They have but they are superfluously ambitious. In marriage, they rely more on reason than on feelings. They give up their with difficulty. Stability and material welfare are the most important for men. They would rather agree to endure wives they do not love than destroy their marriage replacing material with love. Women born in April, however, have different attitude to family life. They appreciate good relations with their husbands, the material side remaining for them in the background. April women are cheerful, witty, and they may find out a reason for merriment in each trifle. Those born in April had better be given names as: Victoria, Andrea, Britney, Kylie, Whitney, Ernest, Andrew, Philip, Oscar, Jonathan.

May

May people are people of principles and uncompromising, domineering and fussy. They may instantly discontinue their relationship and they get easily divorced, though they regret it after that. It is difficult to create a solid family with women born in May, they strive for leadership positions, and they do not endure objections. They are interested in material prosperity most of all, and in events of bad relationships with their husbands, they easily find entertainments beyond their family. Men born in May are good husband, they manage to provide for their families and to obtain the right to be respected. Although with firm nature, they are more yielding in their than out of it. They are greatly influenced by women's tears, complaints, failures. They are always ready to help the fair sex, and this is why they often find themselves in awkward situations. Babies born in May should have names as: Erica, Haley, Sonia, Spencer, Antonio, Patrick, Larry, Kevin.

June

June people are very vulnerable, mistrustful. They are cautious in their deeds, sometimes overplaying safe. They are good and compassionate, but too pigeon-hearted to struggle with anyone. They have many talents by nature, they are practical and enterprising. They are often turned to for advice and moral support. They show their emotions with people close to them rather reservedly, but may be more open with people, whom they do not know so well. They avoid conflicts, at the June men are a little cowardly and weak-willed, when the matter is about personal problems. On that account they are lucky professionally, they are happy in love, in the interest of the truth often out of their family. Amorous by nature, they are easily carried away but not for long. They do not bear moral admonitions and they themselves do not like to preach to people. They are very clean, some of them up to squeamishness. Women know how to create comfort at home and men do their best so that family would not suffer material difficulties. Appropriate names are: Leslie, Brandy, Lauren, Larissa, Valentine, Frank, Dennis, Jimmy, Simon, Martin.

July

Unstable nervous system, impatience, egotism, irritability- these are the characteristic features of July people. They are proud and independent. Egotists. Weak-willed, they may not refuse anything to their friends and they become drunks easily (this refers to men most of all). Women strive for leadership, they try them about the confusion in their families. It is difficult to please them, they are always dissatisfied with something. Men are quite good-natured, carefree, they often make mistakes. As far as women are concerned, they are credulous and naive. If they are deceived once in their feelings, they become confirmed bachelorettes. They endure all troubles in silence, and they do not like to complain of their fate. They may unburden their hearts solely to their mothers, since their mothers are the persons closest to them by soul. Appropriate names are: Judy, Eva, Helen, Mary and Dennis.

August

Too emotional, energetic, persevering. Purposeful in their actions, but not cautious. They do not stand phlegmatic people, who irritate them. August women are confident of their strength, they are not rancorous but they are distrustful. They are leaders in their families. They are good homemakers, but they do not enjoy cooking a lot. Men are sensitive by nature, and they are yielding in their family relationships. They are seldom happy in their first marriage. They do not stand pressure and criticism, they are irritable and expect solely praise and universal acknowledgement. They are very jealous, although they themselves are seldom faithful spouses. They are vulnerable and like children, they require enhanced attention to them from those surrounding them. Appropriate names are: Stacy, Cindy, Caroline, Sabrina, Racheal, Bobby, Markus, Greg, John.

September

Quick-tempered, emotional, purposeful people. They like giving presents, but otherwise not too generous, they would not spend a cent in vain. They try to look open-handed in the eyes of the people surrounding them but they rarely do it without considering their personal interests first. They are calculating and self-centered. Women worry most about themselves than about their husbands, men do not know how to provide for their families, but they will never injure their own feelings. They do not regret losing a great sum of money but if their wives buy expensive garments without their knowledge, they will reproach them of wasting too much money. September people enjoy the company of their friends, but they will never skip their personal benefit even if this is to the detriment of their closes friends. They refund their debts with difficulty and they often forget about them. They do not endure scenes of jealousy, in such events they behave out of spite. They are very jealous themselves. Women are impatient and very independent. They like to sleep until late in the morning and they are often late for work, turning this into something normal. Otherwise, they are wonderful homemakers and everything shines at their homes. They enjoy cooking and are able to cook delicious dishes. Men are too cautious, things come to the contraction of a marriage. Appropriate names are: Kristen, Marissa, Daniel, Julia, Shannon, Mark, Steven, Paul, Peter, Thomas.

October

They are strict, but solely in the events when this refers to their work. They think that it is not always obligatory to be such with their friends. They like to tell fibs and they are witty and enterprising. They are unselfish in the relations with their friends but they are practical and careful in financial operations. They are magnanimous. They do not hurry to draw conclusions and they do not make any rash decisions. They try to listen to as many options as possible, on whose grounds they build up their very close people being of authority for them. Women are objective persons of principles. They have a good memory and easily build up their careers. They do not forgive treasons and betrayal. They try to preserve their families with all their might, where they are leaders and they rarely lean on their on their husbands. Men are practical, sober-minded and a little skinflint. They do not stand criticism, and they are quite good hosts in their families. Appropriate names are: Carmen, Kelly, Linda, Ariel, Henry, Sean, Ryan, Vincent.

November

November people are rather sagacious, being ready to improper deeds because of their personal benefit. They are mercenary and envious. These people are parsimonious, even for those who are closest to them. They do not like, however, being, stingy with themselves. They may leave on holiday with their last money, although their families will have to starve long after that because of it. Women are narcissist, untidy and egotistical. They are leaders in their families and they do not consider their husbands' options into consideration, often being unfaithful to them even not trying to conceal this fact. They are sensuous and they do not choose their partners too much. They select weak-willed men, who have to endure too much from their wives. Men born in November often sink into depression and go through nervous crises. Appropriate names are: Jane, Chelsey, Megan, Pamela, Cody, Jared, Raymond, Gregory, Kenneth.

December

December people are distinguished for their enhanced emotionality, certain instability and quick temper over trifles. They are masters of themselves with being irritated. Moreover, although they perfectly see shortcomings of theirs, and understand the motivations for the sometimes- negative attitude of the people surrounding them, they are not able to restrain themselves. Their lives are arranged in a complicated manner, they often find themselves in unpleasant situations. They cannot and do not know how to live their lives calmly. They sharply need frequent change of the atmosphere, the circle of communication and they do not
Endure monotonous way of living. They are subjected to emotional collapses and depressions. Appropriate names are: Gabriela, Lindsay, Abigail, Olivia, Elizabeth, Brian, Daniel, William.

By Alphabet

Girls Names - A

Name	Meaning	Origin
Abena	Born on Tuesday	African
Abla	Born on Tuesday	African
Adanna	Father's Daughter	African
Adanne	Mother's Daugther	African
Adelaide	Kind	Biblical
Adeline	Noble	Biblical
Afi	Born on Friday	African
Agatha	Good	Biblical
Agnes	Pure	Biblical
Ama	Born on Saturday	African
Anastasia	Resurrection	Biblical
Anna, Anne	From the Hebrew Hanna	Biblical

Abrial, Abrielle, Abril	Open	French
Aimee, Ami, Amie	Loved	French
Alberta	Noble or Bright	French
Amber	Amber	French
Angelique	Form of Angela, which means Angel	French
Antionette	Form of Antonia, which means Flourishing or Praiseworthy	French
Ariane	Arianne	French
Arielle	Form of Ariel, which means Lioness of God	French
Armine	Feminine for Herman	French
Aubrey, Aubree, Aubrie	Blond Ruler	French
Ada	Form of Adelaide	German
Adelaide	Noble and Serene	German
Adelle	Form of Adelaide	German

Anna	Gracious	German
Aubrey	Noble	German
Adrienne	Rich	Greek
Aphrodite, Afrodite	Goddess of Love & Beauty	Greek
Agnes	Pure	Greek
Alcina	Strong Minded	Greek
Alecia, Alesia	Form of Alicia	Greek
Alexandra	Defender of Mankind	Greek
Alexis	Form of Alexandra	Greek
Alice	Truthful	Greek
Alethea	Truth	Greek
Althea	Wholesome	Greek
Anastasia	Resurrection	Greek
Angela	Angel, Messenger	Greek
Athena	Wise	Greek
Aine	Pleasure, Delight	Irish
Aileen	Form of Helen	Irish
Aislinn	Form of Ashlyn	Irish
Alanna (and various	Attractive, Peaceful	Irish

spellings)

Arlene	Pledge	Irish
Ashlyn	Vision, Dream	Irish
Adriana	Form of Adrienne	Italian
Alessandra	Form of Alexandra	Italian
Anna	Gracious	Italian
Aiko	Beloved	Japanese
Akiko	Bright Light	Japanese
Akina	Spring Flower	Japanese
Asa	Born in the Morning	Japanese
Azar, Azara	Fire, Scarlet	Persian
Alina	Beautiful, Bright	Polish
Ania	Form of Hannah	Polish
Adalia	Noble	Spanish
Alameda	Poplar Tree	Spanish
Alegria	Cheerful	Spanish
Alida, Alita	Noble	Spanish
Alva	White	Spanish
Akasma	White Climbing Rose	Turkish

| Azize | Dear, Precious | Turkish |

Girls Names - B

Name	Meaning	Origin
Baba	Born on Thursday	African
Babette	Form of Barbara, meaning stranger	French
Belicia	Dedicated to God	Spanish
Belinda	Beautiful	Spanish
Belle	Beautiful	French
Berget	Form of Bridget	Irish
Bernadette	Form of Bernadine, which means Brave as a Bear	French
Bernadine	Brave as a Bear	German
Bernice	Bringer of Victory	Greek
Bianca, Blanca	White	Italian
Binah	Dancer	African

Binta	With God	African
Bisa	Greatly Loved	African
Blaine	Thin	Irish
Blanche	Form of Bianca	French
Blondelle	Fair Haired	French
Bo	Precious	Chinese
Breck	Freckled	Irish
Brie, Brielle	A region in France known for its cheese	French
Brigette, Bridget	Form of Bridget, which means strong	French
Bryga, Brygida	Form of Bridget	Polish
Bunme, Bunmi	My Gift	African
Belinda	Beautiful	Spanish

Girls Names - C

Name	Meaning
Chiku	Chatterer
Chinue	God's Blessing
Chipo	Gift
Catherine	Pure

Christiana	Female form of Christian
Chu Hua	Chrysanthemum
Cachet	Prestigious
Camille	Young Ceremonial Attendant
Carol	Song of Joy
Cerise, Cera	Cherry
Chalice	Goblet
Chambray	Light Fabric
Chandelle	Candle
Chantal, Chantel, Chante, Shanta	Song
Charmaine	Form of Carmen
Cherry	Cherry Red
Christine	Form of Christina
Colette, Cosette	Form of Nicole
Carla	Farmer
Carol	Farmer
Christa	Form of Christina
Callista	Most Beautiful
Candace, Candice	Glittering White
Cassandra (and all other spellings)	Helper of Men

Cassiopeia	Clever
Cathering (and all other spellings)	Pure
Chloe	Blooming
Christina	Annointed
Clarissa	Brilliant
Cassidy	Clever
Ciara (and various spellings)	Black
Colleen	Girl
Camellia	Evergreen Tree
Camilla	Form of Camille
Capri, Caprice	Fanciful
Carina	Dear Little One
Carlotta	Form of Charlotte
Chiara	Form of Clara
Clarice	Form of Clara
Clarissa	Form of Clara
Concetta	Pure
Chika	Dear
Chiyo	Eternal
Calida	Warm
Catalina	Form of Catherine

Chalina	Form of Rose
Charo	Form of Rosa
Conchita	Conception
Consuelo	Consolation
Corazon	Heart

Girls Names - D

Name	Meaning	Origin
Dalmar	Versatile	African
Damisi	Cheerful	African
Dayo	Joy Arrives	African
Doli	Doll	African
Diana	Moon Goddess	Biblical
Dina	Judgement	Biblical
Donna	Originating from Madonna	Biblical
Danielle	God is My Judge	French
Darci	Fortress	French
Darlene	Little Darling	French
Denise	Follower of Dionysus in	French

	Mythology	
Desiree, Deserae	Desired	French
Destiny	Fate	French
Dior	Golden	French
Dominique	Forms of Dominca, which means belonging to the Lord	French
Delia	Form of Adelaide	German
Danae	From Greek Mythology	Greek
Daphne	Laurel Tree	Greek
Daria	Wealthy	Greek
Demi, Demetria	Cover of the Earth	Greek
Doris, Dorian, Doria	Sea	Greek
Dorothy	Gift of God	Greek
Drew	Courageous	Greek
Dacey	Southerner	Irish
Dacia	Form of Dacey	Irish
Darby	Free	Irish
Darci	Dark	Irish

Name	Meaning	Origin
Deirdre	Sorrowful, Wanderer	Irish
Devan, Devin	Poet	Irish
Daniela	Form of Danielle	Italian
Donna	Lady	Italian
Dai	Great	Japanese
Darya, Daria	Preserver, Sea	Persian
Dulcinea	Sweet	Spanish

Girls Names - E

Name	Meaning	Origin
Efia	Born on Friday	African
Efuru	Daughter of Heaven	African
Elom	God Loves Me	African
Eshe	Life	African
Edna	Pleasure	Biblical
Emma	Healer	Biblical
Evangeline	Good Tidings	Biblical
Elaine	Form of Helen	French
Elita	Choosen	French

Eloise	Form of Louise	French
Evaline	Form of Evelyn	French
Evette, Yvette, Evonne, Yvonne, Ivette, Ivonne	Young Archer	French
Elga	Form of Helga	German
Elke	Form of Alice	German
Elsa	Noble	German
Elsbeth	Form of Elizabeth	German
Elvira	Closed Up	German
Emily	Industrious	German
Emma	Form of Emily	German
Ebony	Hard, Dark Wood	Greek
Eleanor, Ella	Light	Greek
Esmeralda	Form of Emerald	Greek
Eva, Evangelina	Bearer of Good News	Greek
Eileen, Ilene	Form of Helen	Irish
Erin	Peace	Irish
Emilia	Form of Amelia	Italian
Esther	Star	Persian

Name	Meaning	Origin
Elisa	Form of Elizabeth	Spanish
Elvira	Elfin	Spanish
Esmeralda	Form of Emerald	Spanish
Esperanza	Hope	Spanish
Estefani	Form of Stephanie	Spanish
Elma	Sweet Fruit	Turkish

Girls Names - F

Name	Meaning	Origin
Fadhila	Outstanding	African
Faiza	Victorious	African
Farida	Unique	African
Feechi	Worship God	African
Femi	Love Me	African
Faith	Belief & Trust in God	Biblical
Felicity	Happiness	Biblical
Faye	Fairy	French
Fifi	Short for Josephine	French
Fleur	Flower	French

Name	Meaning	Origin
Francine	Form of Frances	French
Frederica	Peaceful Ruler	German
Fallon, Phallon	Grandchild of the Ruler	Irish
Filomena	Form of Philomena	Italian
Francesca	Form of Frances which means Free	Italian
Farah	Joy, Happiness	Persian
Farideh	Unique, Delightful	Persian
Felcia	Lucky	Polish

Girls Names - G

Name	Meaning	Origin
Ghalyela	Precious	African
Gimbya	Princess	African
Grace	Grace	Biblical
Gabrielle	Devoted to God	French
Geneva	Juniper Tree	French
Genevieve, Genovieve, Guinevere	White Wave	French

Genevieve	Form of Guinevere	German
Gertrude	Beloved Warrior	German
Giselle	Pledge	German
Gretchen	Form for Margaret	German
Greta	Form of Gretchen	German
Georgia	Farmer	Greek
Glenna	Valley, Glen	Irish
Gabriela	Form of Gabrielle which means Devoted to God	Italian
Gema	Jewel	Italian
Gianna	Form of Giovanna	Italian
Gina	Short for Angelina	Italian
Giovanna	Form of Jane	Italian
Gen	Spring	Japanese

Girls Names - H

Name	Meaning	Origin
Habika	Sweetheart	African
Haiba	Charm	African
Hanna	Happiness	African
Hamida	Gracious	African
Halla	Unexpected Gift	African
Hannah	Graceful	Biblical
Hope	A virtue	Biblical
Hua	Flower	Chinese
Heidi	Form of Adelaide	German
Helga	Pious	German
Helen, Helena	Light	Greek
Hilary, Hillary	Cheerful	Greek
Hachi	Good Luck	Japanese
Hana	Flower	Japanese
Hisa	Long Lasting	Japanese
Hoshi	Star	Japanese
Hea	Grace	Korean

Hei	Grace	Korean
Hye	Graceful	Korean
Hestia, Hester	Star	Persian

Girls Names - I

Name	Meaning	Origin
Imena	Dream	African
Isabeau, Isabelle	Form of Isabel, which means consecrated to God	French
Ida	Hardworking	German
Imelda	Warrior	German
Ianthe	Violet Flower	Greek
Iola	Dawn	Greek
Iona	Violet Flower	Greek
Irene	Peaceful	Greek
Iris	Rainbow	Greek
Isabella	Form of Isabel	Italian
Ima	Presently	Japanese
Ishi	Rock	Japanese
Isabel	Consecrated to	Spanish

God

Girls Names - J

Name	Meaning	Origin
Jahia	Prominent	African
Jamila	Beautiful	African
Johanna	God's Grace	African
Joy	Pleasure	Biblical
Joyce	Lord	Biblical
Jun	Truthful	Chinese
Jacqueline or Jae	Supplanter, Substitute	French
Jaime, Jamee, Jaimie	I Love	French
Janelle	Form of Jane	French
Jeanette	Form of Jean, which means God is Gracious	French
Jewel	Precious Gem	French
Jolie	Pretty	French
Josephine, Josette	God will add or increase	French

Name	Meaning	Origin
Juliet	Form of Julia, which means Youthful	French
Jillian, Jileen	Youthful, Form of Julia	Irish
Jovanna	Form of Giovanna	Italian
Jasmin, Jasmine	Flower	Persian
Jasia	Form of Jane	Polish
Jolanta	Violet Blossom	Polish
Jacinda	Form of Hyacinth	Spanish
Jade, Jadyn	Jade	Spanish
Josefina	Form of Josephine	Spanish
Juanita	Form of Joan & Jane	Spanish
Juliana	Form of Julia	Spanish

Girls Names - K

Name	Meaning	Origin
Kafi	Quiet	African

Kali	Energetic	African
Kamili	Perfection	African
Kia	Season's Beginning	African
Kari	Pure	Greek
Kyra	Ladylike	Greek
Kaitlin (and various spellings)	Pure, Beautiful	Irish
Kasey, Kasie	Brave	Irish
Keena	Brave	Irish
Kelly (and various spellings)	Brave Warrior	Irish
Kerry	Dark Haired	Irish
Kevyn	Beautiful	Irish
Kiley	Attractive	Irish
Kyla	Attractive	Irish
Kaiya	Forgiveness	Japanese
Kami	Divine Aura	Japanese
Kaya	Resting Place	Japanese
Kei	Reverent	Japanese
Kiaria	Fortunate	Japanese
Kioko	Happy Child	Japanese
Kishi	Happy Life	Japanese

Koko	Stork	Japanese
Kuri	Chestnut	Japanese
Kyoko	Mirror	Japanese
Kasia	Form of Katherine	Polish
Krysta, Krystka	Forms of Krista	Polish

Boys Names - L

Name	Meaning	Origin
Laasya	The Swamp	Spanish
Lada	Goddess of love and fertility	Slavic
Laddona	The Woman	Spanish
Lani	Sky	Hawaiian
Laqueta	The quiet one	African-American
Lara	Cheerful	Greek
Lareina	The Queen	Spanish
Larissa	Cheerful	Greek
Lesley	Grey Fortress	Celtic
Levana	Risen	latin
Licia	Happy	latin

Liesel	Dedicated and gracious	German
Lila	Night	Arabic
Lilianna	Gracious Lily	latin
Lilike	Lily Floewer	Hungarian
Lisle	Of the Iceland	French
Lita	Light	Latin
Louisa	Fight with honer	German
Lovette	Little Loved One	English
Loyal	Faithful, True	English
Lucia	Light	Italian
Lucine	Moonlight	Armenian
Lucky	Fortunate, Light	American
Lyn	Beautiful	American
Lyndsey	Camp near stream	English
Lysandra	One who is freed	Greek

Girls Names - M

Name	Meaning	Origin
Maisha	Life	African
Malika	Queen	African
Madonna	Our Lady	Biblical
Margaret	Jewel	Biblical
Mary	Wished For	Biblical
Meiying, Mei	Beautiful Flower	Chinese
Mallory, Mallorie	Unlucky	French
Mardi	Born on Tuesday	French
Margaux	Form of Margaret	French
Marie	Form of Mary	French
Merle	Blackbird	French
Michelle (and all other spellings)	Who is like God?	French
Mimi	Form of Miriam	French
Monique	Form of Monica	French
Moriah	Dark Skinned	French
Mallory, Malorie	Army Counselor	German

Margret	Form of Margaret	German
Mariel	Form of Mary	German
Madeline (and all other spellings)	High Tower	Greek
Magdalen	High Tower	Greek
Margaret	Pearl	Greek
Marjorie	Form of Margaret	Greek
Maya	Mother	Greek
Melanie	Dark Skinned	Greek
Melinda	Honey	Greek
Monica	Solitary	Greek
Mackenzie	Wise Leader's Daughter	Irish
Megan (and various spellings)	Form of Margaret	Irish
Maura	Dark	Irish
Maureen	Form of Mary	Irish
Muriel	Shining Sea	Irish
Muireann	Sea Fair	Irish
Myrna	Beloved	Irish
Maria	Form of Mary	Italian

Marietta	Form of Marie	Italian
Michele	Form of Michaela	Italian
Mila	Short for Camilla	Italian
Machiko	Fortunate	Japanese
Mai	Brightness	Japanese
Midori	Green	Japanese
Mika	Flower Stem	Japanese
Mina	South	Japanese
Mio	Three Times Strong	Japanese
Miya	Temple	Japanese
Min	Clever	Korean
Mitra	Angel	Persian
Magda	Form of Magdalen	Polish
Margarita	Form of Margaret	Spanish
Maria	Form of Mary	Spanish
Marisol	Sunny Sea	Spanish
Mercedes	Merciful	Spanish

Girls Names - N

Name	Meaning	Origins
Nabila	Noble	African
Nadia	Caller	African
Naima	Graceful	African
Naomi	Merry	Biblical
Natalie	Birthday	Biblical
Nuwa	Mother Goddess	Chinese
Nadia, Nadine	Hopeful	French
Nichole	Victorious People	French
Nora	Light	Greek
Neila	Champion	Irish
Nola	Noble, Famous	Irish
Noreen	Form of Eleanor	Irish
Nami	Wave	Japanese
Nyoko	Gem	Japanese
Nina	Girl	Spanish
Neylan	Fulfilled Wish	Turkish

Girls Names - O

Name	Meaning	Origin
Olympia	Heavenly	Greek
Oriana	Golden	Irish
Oki	Middle of the Ocean	Japanese
Olesia	Defender of Mankind	Polish

Girls Names - P

Name	Meaning	Origin
Paka	Cat	African
Panya	A Twin Child	African
Pulika	Obedience	African
Ping	Duckweed	Chinese
Paris	Capital of France	French
Pamela, Pam	Honey	Greek
Peggy	Form of Margaret	Greek
Peyton	Form of Patricia	Irish
Paola	Form of Paula	Italian

Pia	Devout	Italian
Parveneh	Butterfly	Persian
Patia	Leaf	Spanish
Pilar	Column	Spanish

Girls Names - Q

Name	Meaning	Origin
Qamara	Moon	Arabic
Qi	Fine Jade	Chinese
Qiana	Gracious	American
Quana	Aromatic	Native American
Quanda	A companion	African-American
Quasar	Meteorite	Biblical
Querida	Beloved	Portuguese
Queenie	Queen	American
Questa	Seeking	Latin
Quinta	The fifth	Latin
Quintana	The fifth girl	Latin
Quintessa	Fifth small one	Latin
Quynh	Ruby	Vietnamese
Qwara	Ethiopian Tribe	African

name

Girls Names - R

Name	Meaning	Origin
Rabia	Spring	African
Rafiya	Dignified	African
Raisa	Exalted	African
Reta	Shaken	African
Ridhaa	Goodwill	African
Rachel	Sheep	Biblical
Regina	Queen	Biblical
Raquel	Form of Rachel	French
Renae, Renee	Born Again	French
Riva	River Bank	French
Raina	Mighty	German
Rolanda	Famous in the Land	German
Rhea, Rheanna	Brook	Greek

Name	Meaning	Origin
Reganne, Ragan (and various spellings)	Little Ruler	Irish
Riona	Saint	Irish
Rosa	Form of Rose	Italian
Rosetta	Form of Rose	Italian
Roxann, Roxy	Sunrise	Persian
Ramona	Wise Protector	Spanish
Rosa	Form of Rose	Spanish

Girls Names - S

Name	Meaning	Origin
Saada	Helper	African
Sabra	Patience	African
Saida	Happy	African
Shani	Marvelous	African
Sisi	Born on Sunday	African
Sara, Sarah	Princess	Biblical
Sophia	Knowledge	Biblical
Susan	Kinship	Biblical

Sylvia	Lumber	Biblical
Shanta	Form of Chantal, which means Song	French
Shelley	Form of Michelle	French
Sherry	Beloved	French
Simone	Feminine form of Simon	French
Susette, Suzette	Forms of Susan	French
Selma	Devine Protector	German
Sandra	Defender of Mankind	Greek
Selena, Selina	Moon	Greek
Sonya	Wise	Greek
Stacey (and all other spellings)	Resurrection	Greek
Stephanie (and all other spellings)	Crowned	Greek
Sinead	Form of Jane	Irish
Siobhan	Form of Joan	Irish
Speranza	Form of Esperanza	Italian
Sachi	Blessed	Japanese

Sai	Talented	Japanese
Saki	Cloak	Japanese
Sakura	Wealthy, Prosperous	Japanese
Shika	Gentle Deer	Japanese
Shina	Virtuous	Japanese
Suki	Loved One	Japanese
Sumi	Elegant	Japanese
Suzuki	Bell Tree	Japanese
Sook	Pure	Korean
Sun	Obedient	Korean
Sadira	Lotus Tree, Dreamy	Persian
Shabnam	Dew	Persian
Souzan	Fire	Persian
Savannah	Treeless Plain	Spanish
Soledad	Solitary	Spanish
Sarila	Waterfall	Turkish
Sema	Heaven	Turkish

Girls Names - T

Name	Meaning	Origin
Tabita	Graceful	African
Tawia	Born after Twins	African
Tisha	Strong Willed	African
Theresa	Unknown	Biblical
Tao	Peach	Chinese
Talia	Birthday	French
Tallis	Forest	French
Trudy	Form of Gertrude	German
Tabitha (and all other spellings)	Gazelle	Greek
Talia	Blooming	Greek
Teresa (and all other spellings)	Reaper	Greek
Tiana	Princess	Greek
Trina, Triana	Pure	Greek
Tara	Rocky Hill	Irish
Tierney	Noble	Irish
Trevina	Prudent	Irish
Takara	Treasure	Japanese
Tamika,	Child of the	Japanese

Tamiko	People	
Toki	Hopeful	Japanese
Tori	Bird	Japanese
Toshi	Mirror Image	Japanese
Taraneh	Melody, Song	Persian
Tola	Priceless	Polish
Tia	Aunt	Spanish
Toya	Form of Tory	Spanish

Girls Names - U

Name	Meaning	Origin
Uzima	Vitality	African
Uzuri	Beauty	African
Ushi	Ox	Chinese
Una	Form of Agnes	Irish
Umay	Hopeful	Turkish

Girls Names - V

Name	Meaning	Origin
Valerie	Powerful	Biblical
Vera	Truth	Biblical
Veronica	Genuine Image	Biblical
Vivian	Spirited	Biblical
Violet, Violetta	Purple Flower	French
Virginie	Form of Virginia, which means Pure	French
Vala	Singled Out	German
Velma	Form of Vilhelmina	German
Vanessa	Butterfly	Greek
Venecia	From Venice	Italian
Valencia	Strong	Spanish
Verdad	Truthful	Spanish
Vianca	Form of Bianca	Spanish

Girls Names - W

Name	Meaning	Origin
Wangari	Leopard	African
Winna	Friend	African
Wanda	Wanderer	German
Wilma	Form of Wilhelmina	German
Winifred	Peaceful Friend	German
Winola	Charming Friend	German
Wisia	Form of Victoria	Polish

Girls Names - X

Name	Meaning	Origin
Xiu Mei	Beautiful Plum	Chinese
Xena, Xenia	Hospitable	Greek

Girls Names - Y

Name	Meaning	Origin
Yakini	Truth	African

Yasmin	Jasmine	African
Yobachi	Pray to God	African
Yusra	Ease	African
Yen	Yearning	Chinese
Yin	Silver	Chinese
Yvonne, Yvette	Young Archer	French
Yolanda	Voilet Flower	Greek
Yoko	Good Girl	Japanese
Yoshi	Good	Japanese
Yuki	Snow	Japanese
Yon	Lotus Blossom	Korean

Girls Names - Z

Name	Meaning	Origin
Zalika	Well Born	African
Zawadi	Gift	African
Zina	Secret Spirit	African
Zelma	Form of Selma	German
Zandra	Form of Sandra	Greek
Zoe	Life	Greek
Zola	Piece of Earth	Italian

Zohreh	Happy	Persian
Zosia	Wise	Polish
Zerrin	Golden	Turkish

Boys Names - A

Name	Meaning	Origin
Abel	Second Son of Adam and Eve	Biblical
Abel, Abelard	Noble	German
Abdalla	Servant of God	African
Abdul	Servant of the Lord	African
Abedi	Worshipper	African
Abiola	Born in Honor	African
Abraham	Father of Multitude	Biblical
Achilles	A Trojan War Hero	Greek
Adam	The First Man	Biblical
Adem	Earth	Turkish
Adler	Eagle	German
Adolph	Noble Wolf	German
Adonis	Highly Attractive	Greek

Adrian	Rich	Greek
Afram	A River in Ghana, Africa	African
Aiden	Fiery	Irish
Aimon	House	French
Akira	Intelligent	Japanese
Alaire	Joyful	French
Alaric	Ruler of All	German
Alder	Alder Tree	German
Alec	Form of Alexander	Greek
Alejandro	Form of Alexander	Spanish
Alexander, Alex	Defender of Mankind	Greek
Alexandre	Defender of Mankind	French
Alfonso, Alphonso	Form of Alphonse	Italian
Alfredo	Form of Alfred	Italian
Aloysius	Famous Warrior	German
Alvaro	Just or Wise	Spanish
Alvin	Friend to All	German
Amato	Loved	French

Amir	King	Persian
An	Peaceful	Chinese
Andre	Form of Andrew	French
Andreas	Form of Andrew	Greek
Andres	Form of Andrew	Spanish
Andrew	Manly, Strong	Greek
Andrew	A Strong Man	Biblical
Angelo	Form of Angel	Italian
Anka	Phoenix	Turkish
Ansel	Follower of Noblemen	French
Anthony	Flourishing	Greek
Antione	Form of Anthony	French
Antonio	Form of Anthony	Italian
Aram	Highness	Biblical
Arman	Desire, Hope	Persian
Ata	One of Twins	African
Aubrey	Form of Auberon	French
Aurek	Golden Haired	Polish

| Azizi | Beloved or Precious One | African |

Boys Names - B

Name	Meaning	Origin
Baakir	Eldest	African
Babu	Grandfather	African
Badrani	Full Moon	African
Badru	Born at Full Moon	African
Bahram	A Persian King, Mars Planet	Persian
Bailey, Bayley	Baliff, Steward	French
Bainbridge, Bain	Fair Bridge	Irish
Baldwin	Bold Friend	German
Barak	Thunder	Biblical
Baris	Peaceful	Turkish
Barnabas	Son of Comfort	Biblical
Barrett	Strong as a Bear	German

Basil	Royal	Greek
Beau, Beauregard	Handsome	French
Beaumont	Beautiful Mountain	French
Behrooz, Behrouz	Fortunate, Lucky	Persian
Bello	Helper	African
Benito	Form of Benedict	Italian
Benjiro	Enjoys Peace	Japanese
Benjamin	Son of the Right Hand	Biblical
Benoit	Form of Benedict	French
Berg, Bergen	Mountain, Hill Dweller	German
Berk	Solid	Turkish
Bernard	Brave as a Bear	German
Bernardo	Form of Bernard	Spanish
Bert	Bright and Shining	German
Bishop	Overseer	Greek
Blaine, Blane	Thin	Irish

Name	Meaning	Origin
Blair	Plain, Field	Irish
Bourne	Boundry	French
Boyce	Woods	French
Brian	Strong, Honorable	Irish
Brigham	Brigade	French
Bronislaw	Weapon of Glory	Polish
Bruce	Woods	French
Bruno	Brown Haired	German
Bruno	Brown Haired	Italian
Bryon	Cottage	German

Boys Names - C

Name	Meaning	Origin
Cahil	Young	Turkish
Caleb	Bold	Biblical
Carl	Farmer	German
Carlito, Carlos	Form of Charles	Spanish
Carlo	Form of Carl	Italian
Carmine	Form of Carmel	Italian
Carney	Victorious	Irish

Carsten, Karsten	Annointed	Greek
Casey	Brave	Irish
Casper, Kasper	Treasurer	Persian
Cassius	Protective Cover	French
Chacha	Strong	African
Chadrick	Mighty Warrior	German
Chaney	Oak	French
Channing	Canon	French
Charles	Free Man	Biblical
Charles	Farmer	German
Chase or Chace	Hunter	French
Cheche	Form of Joseph	Spanish
Chen	Great, Tremendous	Chinese
Cheung	Good Luck	Chinese
Chevelier	Horseman	French
Chibale	Kinship	African
Chico	Boy	Spanish
Chidi	God Exists	African
Chiko	Pledge	Japanese
Chimalsi	Proud	African

Christian	A Follower of Christ	Biblical
Christian	Follower of Christ	Greek
Christophe	Form of Christopher	French
Christopher	Holds Christ's Faith	Biblical
Christopher	Christ-Bearer	Greek
Chun	Spring	Chinese
Cisco	Form of Francisco	Spanish
Clancy	Red Headed	Irish
Claus	Form of Nicholas	German
Cleary	Learned	Irish
Clement	Merciful	Biblical
Colin	Form of Nicholas	Greek
Cordell	Rope Maker	French
Cordero	Little Lamb	Spanish
Cortez	Conqueror	Spanish
Cosmo	Roderly, Harmonious	Greek
Coty	Slope	French
Chin	Precious	Korean

Chul	Firm	Korean
Cyrus	Sun	Persian

Boys Names - D

Name	Meaning	Origin
Daktari	Healer	African
Diallo	Bold	African
Donkor	Humble	African
Daniel	God is My Judge	Biblical
David	Beloved	Biblical
Dominic	Belonging to God	Biblical
Dingbang	Protector of the Country	Chinese
Dandre	Combination Name for Andre	French
Darrell, Darryl, Daryl	Beloved	French
Dean	Leader	French

Demont	Mountain	French
Didier	Desired	French
Duke	Leader	French
Derick	Ruler of the People	German
Dieter	Army of the People	German
Dolf	Form of Adolf, meaning Noble Wolf	German
Dustin	Valiant Fighter	German
Damian, Damien	Tamer	Greek
Darius	Wealthy	Greek
Demetrius	Lover of the Earth	Greek
Dennis	From Greek Mythology	Greek
Derry	An Ancient Hero	Irish
Devlin	Brave, Fierce	Irish
Dillon, Dillan	Faithful, Loyal	Irish
Dino	Form of Dean	Italian
Domenico	Form of Dominic	Italian
Danno	Gathering in	Japanese

	the Meadow	
Dobry	Good	Polish
Duman	Misty, Smoky	Turkish

Boys Names - E

Name	Meaning	Origin
Elewa	Intelligent	African
Eze	King	African
Eden	Delight	Biblical
Edward	Successful Leader	Biblical
Eli	Height	Biblical
Elijah	The Lord is My God	Biblical
Eric	Strong Leader	Biblical
Ethan	Loyal	Biblical
Ezekial	God Make Me Stronger	Biblical
Emile	Form of Emil	French
Etienne	Form of Stephen	French

Emery, Emory	Industrious Leader	German
Emmett	Industrious, Strong	German
Engelbert	Bright as an Angel	German
Eric	Form of Frederick, meaning Peaceful Ruler	German
Ernst	Form of Ernest	German
Elias	Form for Elijah	Greek
Eugene	Born to Nobility	Greek
Eagan	Mighty	Irish
Erin	Peaceful	Irish
Evan	Young Warrior	Irish
Emilio	Form of Emil	Italian
Enrico	Form of Henry	Italian
Erek	Lovable	Polish
Emilio	Form of Emil	Spanish
Enrique	Form of Henry	Spanish
Estevan	Form of Stephen	Spanish
Erol	Strong, Courageous	Turkish

Boys Names - F

Name	Meaning	Origin
Fahim	Learned	African
Faraji	Consolation	African
Farhani	Happy	African
Felix	Cheerful	Biblical
Francis	French	Biblical
Fai	Beginning	Chinese
Fontaine	Fountain	French
Forrest or Forest	Forest	French
Fortune	Fortunate	French
Franchot or Francois	Form of Francis	French
Frayne	Dweller at the Ash Tree	French
Frederique	Form of Frederick	French
Faxon	Long Haired	German
Ferdinand	Adventurous	German
Finn	From Finland	German
Franz	Form of Francis	German

Name	Meaning	Origin
Frederick, Friedrich	Peaceful Ruler	German
Fritz	Form of Frederick	German
Fagan	Little Fiery One	Irish
Ferris	Form of Peter, Rock	Irish
Finian	Light Skinned	Irish
Finn	Blond Haired	Irish
Flynn, Flinn	Red Haired Son	Irish
Fabrizio	Craftsman	Italian
Flavio	Form of Flavian meaning yellow haired	Italian
Felipe	Form of Philip	Spanish
Fernando	Form of Ferdinand	Spanish
Frisco	Form of Francisco	Spanish

Boys Names - G

Name	Meaning	Origin
Gamba	Warrior	African
Ghalib	Winner	African

Gabriel	God's Man	Biblical
George	Popular Saint Name	Biblical
Gideon	The Destroyer	Biblical
Giles	Infant Goat	Biblical
Gage	Pledge	French
Gautier	Form of Walter	French
Germain, Jermaine	From Germany	French
Gervaise	Honorable	French
Giles	Goatskin Shield	French
Guillaume	Form of William	French
Gary	Mighty Spearman	German
Gotzon	Form of Angel	German
Guthrie	War Hero	German
Galen, Gale	Healer	Greek
George	Farmer	Greek
Gino	Form of Eugene	Greek
Gannon	Fair Skinned	Irish
Georgio	Form of George	Italian
Geovanni,	Form of John	Italian

Giovanni

Name	Meaning	Origin
Geraldo	Form of Gerald meaning Mighty Spearman	Italian
Giacomo	Form of Jacob	Italian
Giuseppe	Form of Joseph	Italian
Guglielmo	Form of William	Italian
Guido	Form of Guy	Italian
Gustavo	Form of Gustave	Italian
Gerek	Form of Gerard	Polish
Gwidon	Life	Polish
Geraldo	Form of Gerald	Spanish
Giacinto, Jacinto	Hyacinth	Spanish
Guillermo	Form of William	Spanish

Boys Names - H

Name	Meaning	Origin
Haamid	Grateful	African
Habib	Beloved	African
Henry	Lord	Biblical
Ho	Good	Chinese

Hu	Tiger	Chinese
Henri	Form of Henry, Ruler of the House	French
Harvey	Army Warrior	German
Heinrich	Form of Henry	German
Helmut	Courageous	German
Henry	Ruler of the Household	German
Herbert, Herb	Glorious Soldier	German
Herman	Soldier	German
Hector	Steadfast	Greek
Harken	Dark Red	Irish
Hideaki	Clever, Smart	Japanese
Hiroshi	Generous	Japanese
Hisoki	Secretive	Japanese
Hyun-Ki	Wise	Korean
Hyun-Shik	Clever	Korean
Holleb	Dove	Polish
Halil	Dear Friend	Turkish
Hasad	Reaper, Harvester	Turkish

Boys Names - I

Name	Meaning	Origin
Iman	Faith	African
Innis	Island	Irish

Boys Names - J

Name	Meaning	Origin
Jaafar	Small River	African
Jamal	Elegance	African
Juma	Born on Friday	African
Jacob	Son of Isaac	Biblical
James	An Apostle	Biblical
Jason	Healer	Biblical
Jed	God's Friend	Biblical
Joel	The Lord is God	Biblical
John	God is Gracious	Biblical
Johnathan	God's Offering	Biblical
Joseph	God will give more	Biblical
Joshua	God is My	Biblical

	Salvation	
Jin	Gold	Chinese
Jun	Truthful	Chinese
Jacques	Form of Jacob	French
Jontae	Combination Name	French
Jules	Form of Julius	French
Jaegar	Hunter	German
Jarvis	Skilled with a Spear	German
Johan, Johannes	Form of John	German
Jerry	Mighty Spearman	German
Jason	Healer	Greek
Julius, Julian	Youthful	Greek
Jiro	Second Son	Japanese
Joben	Enjoys Cleanliness	Japanese
Juro	Long Life	Japanese
Jerzy	Form of George	Polish
Javier	New House Owner	Spanish
Jose	Form of Joseph	Spanish

Juan	Form of John	Spanish
Juancarlos	Combination of Juan and Carlos	Spanish

Boys Names - K

Name	Meaning	Origin
Kamuzu	Medicinal	African
Kosey	Lion	African
Kong	Glorious	Chinese
Kueng	Universe	Chinese
Kurt, Curt	Courteous	French
Keene, Keane	Bold, Sharp	German
Kurt	Courteous	German
Khristos, Christos	Form of Christopher	Greek
Keanu	Form of Keenan	Irish
Kyle	Narrow Piece of Land	Irish
Kane	Golden	Japanese
Kaori	Strong	Japanese
Kentaro	Big Boy	Japanese

Name	Meaning	Origin
Kin	Golden	Japanese
Kioshi	Quiet	Japanese
Kemal	Highest Honor	Turkish
Kerem	Noble, Kind	Turkish
Khan	Prince	Turkish

Boys Names - L

Name	Meaning	Origin
Latif	Gentle	African
Lawrence	From Laurentum	Biblical
Louis	Famous warrior	Biblical
Luke	Author of the Gospel of Saint Luke	Biblical
Luther	Soldier of the people	Biblical
Liang	Good	Chinese
Lafayette	Historical French Soldier	French
Lamar	Sea, Ocean	French
Lamond	World	French
Laurent	Form of Laurence	French

Leroy	King	French
Lyle	Island	French
Lamar	Famous in the Land	German
Lance	Form of Lancelot	German
Leonard	Brave as a Lion	German
Louis	Famous Warrior	German
Leon, Leonard	Brave as a Lion	Greek
Liam	Unwavering Protector	Irish
Lynch	Mariner	Irish
Lazaro	Form of Lazarus	Italian
Leonardo	Form of Leonard	Italian
Luciano	Form of Lucian	Italian
Luigi	Form of Louis	Italian
Liuz	Light	Polish
Luboslaw	Lover of Glory	Polish
Lorenzo	Form of Lawrence	Spanish

Boys Names - M

Name	Meaning	Origin
Maalik	Experienced	African
Moswen	Light in Color	African
Muhammed	Praised	African
Malcolm	Disciple	Biblical
Mark	Author of the Gospel According to Saint Mark	Biblical
Matthew	God's Gift	Biblical
Michael	Archangel	Biblical
Moses	Drawn out of the Water	Biblical
Manchu	Pure	Chinese
Marc	Form of Mark	French
Marcel	Form of Marcellus	French
Marquis	Nobleman	French
Marshall	Horse Caretaker	French
Mason	Stone Worker	French
Michel	Form of Michael	French
Montague	Pointed	French

	Mountain	
Montrell or Montreal	Royal Mountain	French
Macon	Maker	German
Mauritz	Form of Maurice	German
Miles	Merciful	German
Milo	Form of Miles	German
Milos	Pleasant	Greek
Moris	Son of the Dark One	Greek
Myron	Fragrant Ointment	Greek
Marcelo	Form of Marcellus	Italian
Marciano	Form of Martin	Italian
Marco	Form of Marcus	Italian
Milan	Northerner	Italian
Makoto	Sincere	Japanese
Mareo	Uncommon	Japanese
Masao	Righteous	Japanese
Masato	Just	Japanese
Miki	Tree	Japanese
Mehrdad	Gift of the Sun	Persian

Mandek	Army Man	Polish
Marcin	Form of Martin	Polish
Miron	Peace	Polish
Marcos	Form of Marcus	Spanish
Miguel	Form of Michael	Spanish

Boys Names - N

Name	Meaning	Origin
Naasir	Defender	African
Nanji	Safe	African
Nassor	Victorious	African
Nathan	God's Gift	Biblical
Noah	Peaceful, Restful	Biblical
Noel	Christ's Birthday	French
Nemo	Glen	Greek
Nickolas (and all other spellings)	Victorious People	Greek
Nevan	Holy	Irish

Name	Meaning	Origin
Napoleon	From Naples	Italian
Nuncio	Messenger	Italian
Naoko	Honest	Japanese
Natan	God has Given	Polish
Nardo	Form of Bernardo	Spanish
Nero	Stern	Spanish

Boys Names - O

Name	Meaning	Origin
Odongo	Second of Twins	African
Ochi	Laughter	African
Ohin	Chief	African
Olivier	Form of Oliver	French
Otis	Son of Otto	German
Othman	Wealthy	German
Otto	Rich	German
Ohannes	Form of John	Turkish
Onan	Prosperous	Turkish
Osman	Ruler	Turkish

Boys Names - P

Name	Meaning	Origin
Paki	Witness	African
Patrick	Nobleman	Biblical
Paul	Small	Biblical
Peter	Stone	Biblical
Philip	Horse Lover	Biblical
Po Sin	Grandfather Elephant	Chinese
Page	Youthful Assistant	French
Philippe	Form of Philip	French
Pierre	Form of Peter	French
Paris	Lover	Greek
Peter	Small Rock	Greek
Philip, Phil	Horse Lover	Greek
Paddy	Form of Patrick, Nobleman	Irish
Patterson	Son of Pat	Irish
Pasquale	For of Pascal	Italian
Pablo	Form of Paul	Spanish
Paco	Form of Francisco	Spanish

Paz	Solitary	Spanish
Pedro	Form of Peter	Spanish
Pepe	Form of Joseph	Spanish

Boys Names - Q

Name	Meaning	Origin
Quon	Bright	Chinese
Quinlan, Quinn	Strong	Irish

Boys Names - R

Name	Meaning	Origin
Rafiki	Friend	African
Rashad	Righteous	African
Rasul	Messenger	African
Richard	Great Strength	Biblical
Raoul or Raul	Form of Ralph	French
Rene	Reborn	French
Roy	King	French
Russell	Redhead	French

Roderick	Famous Ruler	German
Roger	Famous Spearman	German
Rolf	Form of Ralph	German
Rory	Form of Roderick	German
Rudolf	Famous Wolf	German
Roland, Rowland	Famous in the Land	German
Reilly, Riley	Valiant	Irish
Rian, Ryan	Little King	Irish
Raimondo	Form of Raymond	Italian
Renardo	Form of Reynard	Italian
Rinaldo	Form of Reynold	Italian
Rocco	Rock	Italian
Romeo	Pilgrim to Rome	Italian
Rudolpho	Form of Rudolph	Italian
Raiden	The Thunder God	Japanese
Renjiro	Virtuous	Japanese
Ringo	Apple	Japanese

Name	Meaning	Origin
Ramin	Warrior	Persian
Raimundo, Ramon	Form of Raymond	Spanish
Ricardo, Rico	Form of Richard	Spanish
Rusk	Twisted Bread	Spanish
Rafal	Form of Raphael	Polish
Rufin	Red Head	Polish

Boys Names - S

Name	Meaning	Origin
Saad	Good Fortune	African
Salim	Peaceful	African
Said	Happy	African
Salaam	Peach	African
Senwe	Dry Grain Stalk	African
Sampson	Child of the Sun	Biblical
Stephen	Protected	Biblical
Shen	Meditation	Chinese
Shing	Victory	Chinese
Sidney, Sydney	From St. Denis,	French

	France	
Sinclair	Prayer	French
Siegfried	Victorious Peace	German
Sigmund	Victorious Protector	German
Sebastian (and all other spellings)	Venerable	Greek
Spiro	Breath, Round Basket	Greek
Stamos	Form of Stephen	Greek
Stephen (and all other spellings)	Crowned	Greek
Seamus, Shamus	One who supplants	Irish
Shane	God is Gracious	Irish
Sergio	Form of Serge	Italian
Silvio	Form of Silvan	Italian
Stefano	Form of Stephan	Italian
Saburo	Third Born Son	Japanese
Samuru	Form of Samuel	Japanese

Name	Meaning	Origin
Shiro	Fourth Born Son	Japanese
Soo	Excellence	Korean
Sun	Goodness	Korean
Shah	King	Persian
Sohrab	A Hero	Persian
Soroush	Messenger	Persian
Santiago, Yago	Form of James	Spanish
Sevilen	Beloved	Turkish

Boys Names - T

Name	Meaning	Origin
Tahir	Pure	African
Taji	Crown	African
Talib	Seeker	African
Thomas	Identical	Biblical
Tobias	The Lord is Kind	Biblical
Tempest	Stormy	French
Thibault	Form of Theobald	French
Tyson	Son of Ty	French

Name	Meaning	Origin
Terrell	Thunder Ruler	German
Traugott	God's Truth	German
Thaddeus, Tad	Courageous	Greek
Thanos	Nobleman	Greek
Theodore	Gift of God	Greek
Timothy	Honoring God	Greek
Tyrone	Sovereign	Greek
Teagan	Attractive	Irish
Torin	Chief	Irish
Tomasso	Form of Thomas	Italian
Taro	First Born Son	Japanese
Tomi	Rich	Japanese
Tanek	Immortal	Polish
Tiago	Form of Jacob	Spanish
Tabib	Physician	Turkish

Boys Names - U

Name	Meaning	Origin
Ubora	Excellence	African
Umar	Longevity	African
Ulan	First Born Twin	African

Ulrich	Wolf Ruler	German
Umberto	Form of Humbert	Italian
Udo	Ginseng Plant	Japanese
Umit	Hope	Turkish

Boys Names - V

Name	Meaning	Origin
Valentine	Powerful	Biblical
Victor	Winner	Biblical
Vincent	To Occupy	Biblical
Victoir	Form of Victor	French
Vilhelm, Vasyl	Form of William	German
Von	Unknown	German
Valentino	Form of Valentin which means Strong	Italian
Vincenzo	Form of Vincent which means Victor	Italian

Boys Names - W

Name	Meaning	Origin
Waitimu	Born of the Spear	African
William	Strenuous Guardian	Biblical
Wang	Hope, Wish	Chinese
Wing	Glory	Chinese
Walter	Army ruler	German
Warren	General	German
Wendell	Wanderer	German
Wilfred	Determined Peacemaker	German
Wolfgang	Wolf Quarrel	German
Wit	Life	Polish

Boys Names - X

Name	Meaning	Origin
Xander	Form of Alexander	Greek
Xenos	Stranger	Greek
Xerxes	Ruler	Persian

Boys Names - Y

Name	Meaning	Origin
Yohance	God's Gift	African
Yong	Courageous	Chinese
Yu	Universe	Chinese
Yves	Form of Ives	French
Yanni, Yanny, Yannis	Form of John	Greek
Yasashiku	Polite, Gentle	Japanese
Yoshi	Adopted	Japanese

Boys Names - Z

Name	Meaning	Origin
Zahir	Shining	African
Zesiro	Elder of Twins	African
Zuri	Good Looking	African
Zareb	Protector	African
Zander	Form of Alexander	Greek
Zeno	Cart, Harness	Greek
Zen	Religious	Japanese
Zinan	Second Son	Japanese

| Zarek | May God Protect the King | Polish |
| Zeki | Clever, Intelligent | Turkish |

Made in the USA
Charleston, SC
12 June 2011